TOM GLAZER'S CHRISTMAS SONGBOOK

TOM GLAZER'S CHRISTMAS SONGBOOK

BY TOM GLAZER

ILLUSTRATED BY BARBARA CORRIGAN

A Doubleday Book for Young Readers

DOUBLEDAY BOOKS FOR YOUNG READERS BY TOM GLAZER

Eye Winker Tom Tinker Chin Chopper: Fifty Musical Fingerplays
Mother Goose Songbook
Music for Ones and Twos: Songs and Games for the Very Young Child
Tom Glazer's Christmas Songbook
Tom Glazer's Treasury of Songs for Children

A Doubleday Book for Young Readers

Published by Delacorte Press, Bantam Doubleday Dell Publishing Group, Inc.
666 Fifth Avenue, New York, New York 10103

Doubleday and the portrayal of an anchor with a dolphin are trademarks of
Bantam Doubleday Dell Publishing Group, Inc.

Library of Congress Cataloging-in-Publication Data
Tom Glazer's Christmas songbook.
    Summary: Presents a collection of forty favorite Christmas songs and carols.
Includes piano and guitar accompaniment.
    1. Carols, English.   2. Christmas music.
[1. Carols.   2. Christmas music]   I. Glazer, Tom.
II. Corrigan, Barbara, 1922–   ill.   III. Title:
Christmas songbook.
M2065.T65   1989   88-751568
ISBN 0-385-24641-2

Original piano/guitar arrangements
Copyright © 1989 by Tom Glazer, Songs Music, Inc., Scarborough, N.Y. 10510
Illustrations Copyright © 1989 by Barbara Corrigan

DESIGNED BY/DIANE STEVENSON/SNAP • HAUS GRAPHICS

ACKNOWLEDGMENTS

"I Heard the Bells on Christmas Day," music by Johnny Marks, lyrics by Henry Wadsworth Longfellow, adapted by Johnny Marks, copyright © 1956 St. Nicholas Music Inc., 1619 Broadway, New York, NY 10019, Renewed 1984. All rights reserved. Reprinted by permission.

"I'll Be Home for Christmas," words by Kim Gannon; music by Walter Kent, © 1943 and renewed 1971 by Gannon & Kent Music Co., Beverly Hills, CA. All rights reserved. Reprinted by permission.

"A Christmas Present To Santa Claus," "O Christmas Tree", "Little Bitty Baby," and, "Patapan" adapted with original lyrics by Tom Glazer, © 1987–88 Songs Music, Inc., Scarborough, NY 10510. Reprinted by permission.

"Rudolph the Red-Nosed Reindeer," music and lyrics by Johnny Marks, copyright © 1949 St. Nicholas Music Inc., 1619 Broadway, New York, NY 10019, Renewed 1977. All rights reserved. Reprinted by permission.

While every effort has been made to obtain permission, there may still be cases in which we have failed to trace a copyright holder, and we would like to apologize for any apparent negligence.

To children and grownups and practically everyone else:
*My best of wishes for your Merry Christmases and
your Happy New Years, your long lives and your
true prosperities.*

        —Charles Dickens

CONTENTS

INTRODUCTION

At Christmas play and make good cheer,
For Christmas comes but once a year.
                                    —Thomas Tusser, 1557

Christmas without music would be like a birthday without presents. It is impossible to think of the holiday without carols and appropriate hymns, and Handel's *Messiah* and Bach's great *Christmas Oratorio,* a chorale from which is in this book—"Break Forth, O Beauteous Heavenly Light."

This is a collection of most of the best-loved Christmas songs and carols, ranging from the most ancient to the more recent, popular Christmas songs. Of course, all the songs herein are popular in another sense. It goes without saying that I also mean by "popular" those songs that have found great favor in English-speaking countries—most of Anglo-American origin, but some from foreign lands. I regret the possible exclusion of a few favorites, but one will find most of the familiar ones and a few lovely examples of some not too familiar, and even unfamiliar.

I have tried to make the piano arrangements easy to play without sacrificing musicality, while retaining a few time-tested arrangements—especially one or two settings by famous composers, such as Bach's chorale from the *Christmas Oratorio* and a fine song by Gustav Holst. However, I always feel that amateur pianists or guitarists should not be intimidated by anything found herein. Amateur pianists should simplify difficult passages, while accomplished pianists should amplify if they find passages too simple. And guitarists who find some chords unfamiliar or hard can use a capo to transpose to simpler keys; or they can alter ninth chords to sevenths, or minor seventh chords to simple minors. As for keys, in almost all cases I have kept singing ranges toward midregisters; exceptions are where I wanted to keep either simpler key signatures or a famous composer's original key.

Christmas memories! How sweet and bittersweet they are; we all have them. Mine go back many, many years to when I accompanied my Catholic classmate and close friend, Bill Smith, to Midnight Mass on a very cold Christmas Eve. It was too crowded to get into the Cathedral on the Parkway in midtown Philadelphia but the doors were wide open. We listened and watched as best we could standing outside, hearing the music and the noble cadences of the Mass in Latin.

Or later, in New York, how exhilarating the season was; I could not prevent myself from becoming almost overexcited. The cold, the hurrying crowds, the decorations, the prospect of days off from work, the parties, the presents given and received, the good cheer, the lights all over town. People seemed happier. I know I was.

And later still, living in the country, going wassailing on Christmas Eve, as some of us did for several years, adults and children on clear or snowy nights.

Or at midnight one Christmas Eve, walking alone down the still streets of Farringdon, in Hampshire, England, to the one church in that small town to attend the service, and then walking back to the house I was visiting, again alone, everything totally quiet, a brilliantly clear night, the stars gleaming overhead. "It came upon the midnight clear, that glorious song of old."

So here are these glorious songs of old—of old yet always new, like Christmas itself. Except for the Old Testament Golden Rule to love one's neighbor as oneself, there is no more beautiful and necessary sentiment than the message of Christmas: "peace on earth, good will to men," meaning men, women, and children, and everyone. And I do mean everyone.

—Tom Glazer
Stillwater Lake
Newcastle, New York
Winter 1988

TOM GLAZER'S CHRISTMAS SONGBOOK

ANGELS, FROM THE REALMS OF GLORY

James Montgomery was an Irishman who was born in Scotland and was orphaned early in life. After various odd jobs he became a newspaperman and editor and writer of hymns, several of which are found in Protestant hymnals. He was a "premature" fighter against slavery and was once jailed for writing a poem that praised the fall of the Bastille in the French Revolution. The tune was written thirteen years after Montgomery's death.

1. An - gels from the realms of glo - ry, Wing your flight o'er
2. Shep - herd in the field a - bid - ing, Watch - ing o'er your

all the earth; Ye who sang cre - a - tion's sto - ry,
flocks by night; God with man is now re - sid - ing,

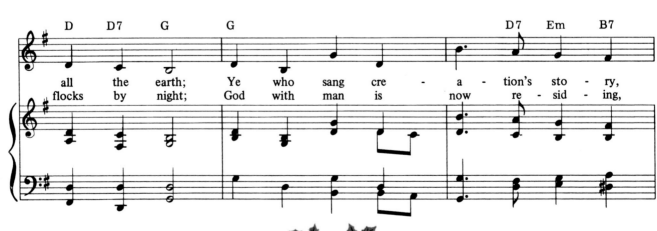

Now pro - claim Mes - si - ah's birth.
Yon - der shines the_____ in - fant light.}
Come and wor - ship,

Come and wor - ship, wor - ship Christ the new - born King.

3. Sages, leave your contemplations,
Brighter visions beam afar.
Seek the great desire of nations;
Ye have seen His natal star.
(Chorus)

AWAY IN A MANGER

Often incorrectly ascribed to Martin Luther. The words first appeared in *Little Children's Book,* published by the Evangelical Lutheran Church in North America in 1885. James R. Murray may have been the composer of the tune—it isn't certain—and many other melodies have been written to the words. This tune is the most famous, but the melody of "Flow Gently, Sweet Afton" is also heard and used.

1. A - way in a man - ger, no crib for a bed, The lit - tle Lord
2. The cat - tle are low - ing, the poor ba - by wakes, But lit - tle Lord

Je - sus laid down His sweet head. The stars in the sky_____ looked
Je - sus, no cry - ing He makes. I love Thee, Lord Je - sus, look

down where He lay, The lit - tle Lord Je - sus, a - sleep on the hay.
down from the sky, And stay by my side un - til morn - ing is nigh.

BREAK FORTH, O BEAUTEOUS HEAVENLY LIGHT

This great chorale is from Bach's *Christmas Oratorio.* It is sung just after a recitative from St. Luke: "And there were shepherds in the same country . . ." The words were written by a minister, Johann Rist, in 1641 in Germany, and the melody by another Johann, Schop. Bach's melody is not identical to Schop's, though based on it.

Break forth, O beau-teous heaven-ly light, and ush-er in the

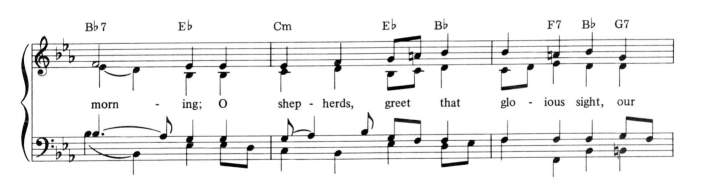

morn - ing; O shep-herds, greet that glo - ious sight, our

Lord a crib a - dorn - ing. This child, this lit - tle

BRING A TORCH, JEANNETTE, ISABELLA

Some scholars place this French carol in Provence, in the seventeenth century, perhaps written by one Nicholas Saboly. The fine English words were written by a British composer and organist who died in 1914, E. C. Nunn.

1. Bring a torch,__ Jean - nette, Is a - bel - la, Bring a
2. It is wrong when the child __ is sleep - ing, It is

torch, to the cra - dle run. It is Je - sus, good
wrong __ to talk __ so loud. Si - lence all, as you

folk of the vil - lage, Christ___ is born, and Mar - y's
gath - er a - round,_____ Lest___ your noise and should wak - en

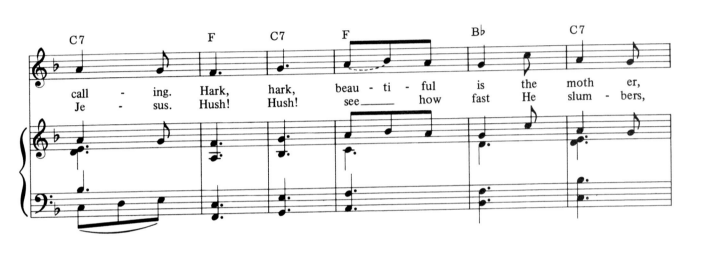

call - ing. Hark, hark, beau - ti - ful is the moth - er,
Je - sus. Hush! Hush! see___ how fast He slum - bers,

Hark, hark, beau - ti - ful is the child._____
Hush! Hush! see___ how fast He sleeps.

3. Softly to the little stable,
Softly for a moment come;
Look and see how charming is Jesus,
How He is white, His cheeks are rosy!
Hush! Hush! see how the child is sleeping;
Hush! Hush! see how He smiles in dreams.

THE CHERRY TREE CAROL

The great British folklorist, collector, and arranger Cecil Sharp toured our southern Appalachians in 1916–18 and collected some 273 ballads and songs of English origin. (Sharp, it is said, rather cavalierly dismissed native American folk songs as inferior, like spirituals and cowboy songs; it was left to later, American collectors to mine this great treasure.) Mr. Sharp collected 6 versions of this beautiful, charming folk song. I have adapted the tune of one version to the words of another.

1. When Jo - seph was a young__ man, a young man was__ he, He__ court - ed Vir - gin Mar - y, the Queen of Gal - i - lee, He__ court - ed Vir - gin Mar - y, the Queen of Gal - i - lee.

2. Then Mar - y spoke a few__ words, so meek and so__ mild, "Jo - seph, gath - er me some cher - ries, for I am with__ child, Jo - seph, gath - er me some cher - ries, for I am with__ child."

3. Then Joseph flew in anger, in anger flew he:
"Let the father of thy baby gather cherries for thee.
Let the father of thy baby gather cherries for thee."

4. Then Jesus spoke a few words, a few words spoke He:
"Let my mother have some cherries; bow low down, cherry tree.
Let my mother have some cherries; bow low down, cherry tree."

5. The cherry tree bowed low down, bowed low down to the ground,
And Mary had some cherries, while Joseph stood around,
And Mary had some cherries, while Joseph stood around.

6. Then Joseph took Mary all on his left knee:
"What have I done, Lord; have mercy on me.
What have I done, Lord; have mercy on me."

7. Then Joseph took Jesus all on his right knee:
"Go and tell me, pretty baby, when Thy birthday will be.
Go and tell me, pretty baby, when Thy birthday will be."

8. "On the sixth day of January, My birthday will be,
When the stars in their elements shall tremble with glee,
When the stars in their elements shall tremble with glee."

CHRISTMAS IS COMING

The custom still prevails in this country for panhandlers to say "God bless you" rather sarcastically, especially when turned down. Perhaps this tone is also expressed by the olden-times English beggars when they say in the song, "If you don't have a ha'penny, then God bless you." Sing it as is or as a round in three parts, as indicated.

A CHRISTMAS PRESENT TO SANTA CLAUS

WORDS AND MUSIC BY TOM GLAZER

Rosemary Clooney recorded this in 1954. As the world turns, Santa has yet to receive his present of "peace and love on earth forevermore." But the hope for it at Christmas and year round endures.

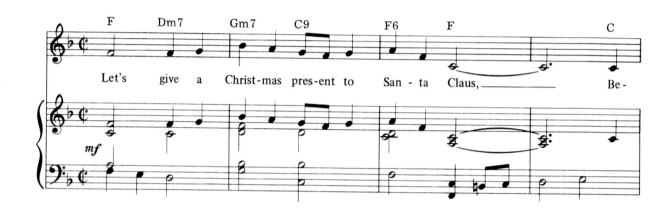

Let's give a Christ-mas pres-ent to San-ta Claus,_____ Be-

cause we love him so,_____ And what would you sug-

gest to please dear San-ta best? Since he owns most ev-'ry toy,

what do you think would bring him joy? Let's give a Christ-mas pres-ent to

San - ta Claus,_____ Be - cause he's kind and

good._____ Late last night when the world was still, I

dreamed he sat on my win-dow-sill, and said, "The Christ-mas gift I'm hop-ing

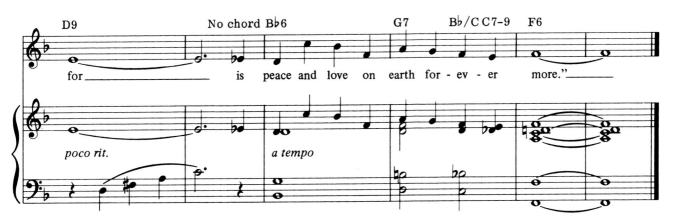

for _____ is peace and love on earth for - ev - er more." _____

DECK THE HALLS

All we know of this, one of the most popular of all carols, is that it's of Welsh origin, and that it caught the attention of Mozart himself, who used the melody in a piano-violin duet.

1. Deck the halls with boughs of ___ hol - ly,
2. See the blaz - ing Yule be - fore us,

Fa la la la la la la la la. 'Tis the sea - son
Strike the harp, and

to be ___ jol - ly,
join the ___ cho - rus,

Fa la la la la la la la la.

3. Fast away the old year passes,
Fa la la la la la la la la
Hail the new! ye lads and lasses;
Fa la la la la la la la la
Sing we joyous all together,
Fa la la la la la la la la
Heedless of the wind and weather,
Fa la la la la la la la la.

34

THE FIRST NOEL

The earliest known version appeared in print probably in 1833. Experts place its origin about two hundred years before that, however.

1. The ___ first ___ No - el, the ___ an - gel did
2. They ___ look - ed up and ___ saw ___ a

say, Was to cer - tain poor shep - herds in fields as they
star, Shin - ing in ___ the east be - yond ___ them

3. And by the light of that same star
Three wise men came from country far;
To seek for a King was their intent,
And to follow the star wherever it went.
(Chorus)

4. This star drew nigh to the northwest;
O'er Bethlehem it took its rest;
And there it did both stop and stay,
Right over the place where Jesus lay.
(Chorus)

5. Then entered in those wise men three,
Full reverently upon the knee,
And offered there, in His presence,
Their gold and myrrh and frankincense.
(Chorus)

THE FRIENDLY BEASTS

As the result of extensive research conducted by the author twenty-five years ago, the following was discovered, as I wrote then: It is not a twelfth-century English carol, as more books are declaring, borrowing the same mistake. The tune is an old French carol, "Orientis Partibus" (in Eastern—that is, Mideastern—lands), revived by the British hymnist Richard Redhead in the 1850s. The words are by Robert Davis, onetime assistant minister of the Brick Presbyterian Church of New York, who wrote it for a Christmas pageant of Dr. Clarence Dickenson, organist of the church in the early 1900s. Davis left the Brick under a mysterious cloud and died during World War I.

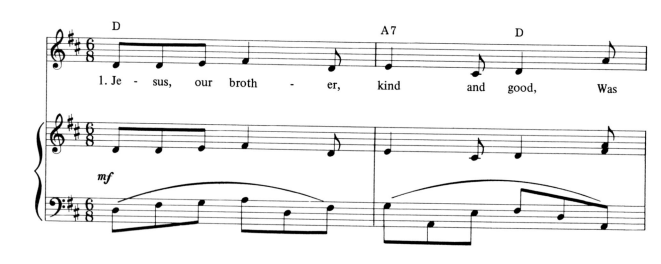

1. Je - sus, our broth - er, kind and good, Was

hum - bly born in a sta - ble rude, And the friend - ly beasts a-

round Him stood, Je - sus, our broth - er, kind and good.

2. "I," said the donkey, shaggy and brown,
"I carried His mother up hill and down;
I carried His mother to Bethlehem town.
I," said the donkey, shaggy and brown.

4. "I," said the sheep with curly horn,
"I gave Him my wool for His blanket warm.
I gave Him my coat on Christmas morn.
I," said the sheep with curly horn.

3. "I," said the cow, all white and red,
"I gave Him my manger for His bed;
I gave Him my hay for to rest His head.
I," said the cow, all white and red.

5. Thus ev'ry beast by some good spell
In the stable dark was glad to tell
Of the gift he gave Emmanuel,
Of the gift he gave Emmanuel.

GO TELL IT ON THE MOUNTAIN

Since music is mostly, perhaps always, an untranslatable language, it is virtually impossible to convey in words just how or why spirituals are so moving: to mention simplicity, deep feeling, unsophisticated poetic utterance expresses a little of the genius of the black spiritual. As with innumerable folk songs, we know nothing of the author or composer of this Christmas spiritual, one of the greatest.

GOD REST YOU MERRY, GENTLEMEN

I am sure I made the same error for many years that millions of children have made: thinking of the words as "God rest you, merry gentlemen," instead of placing the comma after "merry." Dickens mentions the carol in *A Christmas Carol*.

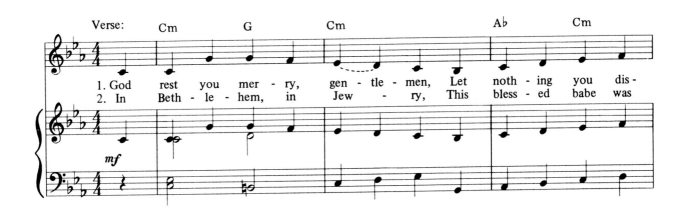

1. God rest you mer - ry, gen - tle - men, Let noth - ing you dis -
2. In Beth - le - hem, in Jew - ry, This bless - ed babe was

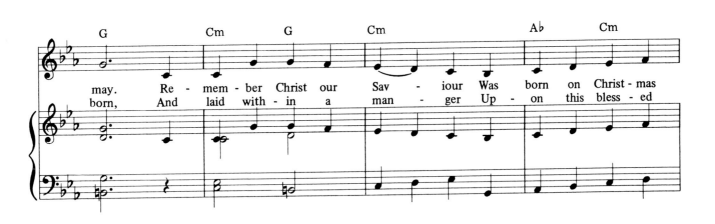

may. Re - mem - ber Christ our Sav - iour Was born on Christ - mas
born, And laid with - in a man - ger Up - on this bless - ed

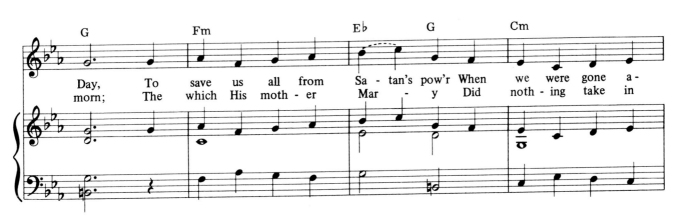

Day, To save us all from Sa - tan's pow'r When we were gone a -
morn; The which His moth - er Mar - y Did noth - ing take in

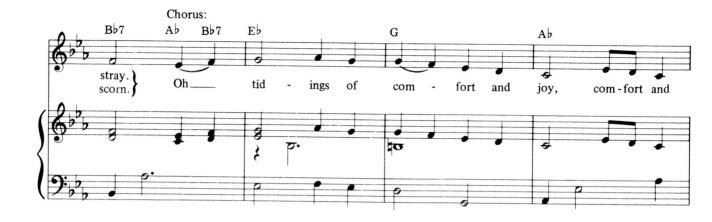

Chorus:

stray.
scorn.
Oh___ tid - ings of com - fort and joy, com-fort and

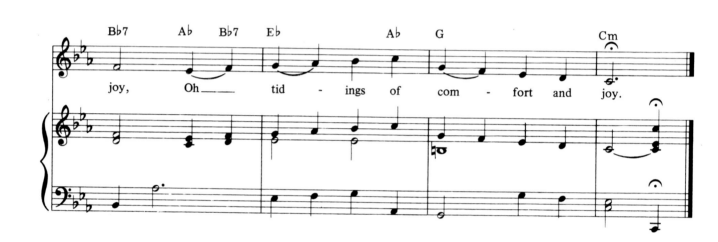

joy, Oh___ tid - ings of com - fort and joy.

3. From God our heav'nly Father
A blessed angel came:
And unto certain shepherds
Brought tidings of the same:
How that in Bethlehem was born
The Son of God by name.
(Chorus)

4. "Fear not, then," said the angel,
"Let nothing you affright,
This day is born a Saviour
Of a pure Virgin bright,
To free all those who trust in Him
From Satan's power and might."
(Chorus)

5. The shepherds at those tidings
Rejoiced much in mind,
And left their flocks a-feeding,
In tempest, storm and wind,
And went to Bethl'em straightway
This blessed babe to find.
(Chorus)

6. But when to Bethlehem they came,
Whereat this infant lay,
They found Him in a manger,
Where oxen feed on hay;
His mother Mary kneeling
Unto the Lord did pray.
(Chorus)

7. Now to the Lord sing praises,
All you within this place,
And with true love and brotherhood
Each other now embrace;
This holy tide of Christmas
All others doth deface.
(Chorus)

8. God bless the ruler of this house,
And send him long to reign,
And many a merry Christmas
May live to see again;
Among your friends and kindred
That live both far and near—
And God send you a happy new year, happy new year,
And God send you a happy new year.

GOOD KING WENCESLAS

Wenceslas (Wenzel) was a ruler of Bohemia (now part of Czechoslovakia) in the tenth century, whose good deeds were so outstanding that he was made a saint. The tune originally was a song of spring, appearing in the 1500s. Whether the story actually occurred is uncertain; what is certain is that John M. Neale's words to a great tune is a most felicitous collaboration.

1. Good King Wen - ces - las looked out   On the feast of   Ste - phen
2. "Hith - er page, and   stand by me,   If thou knows't it   tell - ing.

When the snow lay round a - bout,   Deep and crisp and   e - ven.
Yon - der peas - ant, who is   he?   Where and what his   dwell - ing?"

Bright - ly shone the   moon that night,   Though the frost was   cru - el,
"Sire, he lives a   good league hence,   Un - der - neath the   moun - tain,

When a poor man   came in sight   Gath - 'ring win - ter   fu - el.
Right a - gainst the   for - est fence   By St. Ag - nes'   foun - tain."

3. "Bring me flesh, and bring me wine;
Bring me pine logs hither.
Thou and I shall see him dine
When we bear them thither."
Page and monarch forth they went;
Forth they went together,
Through the rude wind's wild lament
And the bitter weather.

4. "Sire, the night is darker now,
And the wind grows stronger;
Fails my heart, I know not how;
I can go no longer."
"Mark my footsteps, my good page,
Tread thou in them boldly;
Thou shalt find the winter's rage
Freeze thy blood less coldly."

5. In his master's steps he trod,
Where the snow lay dinted;
Heat was in the very sod
Which the saint had printed.
Therefore, Christian men, be sure,
Wealth or rank possessing,
Ye who now will bless the poor
Shall yourselves find blessing.

HARK! THE HERALD ANGELS SING

This is a most interesting, and rather rare, example of a third party, a William Cummings, taking the words of a first party—Charles Wesley, one of the pioneers of Methodism—and marrying them to the tune of a second party, the famous composer Felix Mendelssohn; neither Wesley nor Mendelssohn ever during their lives learned that this was to be done.

1. "Hark!" the her - ald an - gels sing,____ "Glo - ry to the
2. Christ by high - est heav'n a - dored;____ Christ the Ev - er -

new - born King; Peace on earth and mer - cy mild,____
last - ing Lord; Come, De - sire of na - tions, come,____

God and sin - ners rec - on - ciled!" Joy - ful all ye
Fix in us Thy hum - ble home. Veiled in flesh the

na - tions rise;_____ Join the tri - umph of the skies;_____
God - head see;_____ Hail the In - car - nate De - i - ty,_____

With th' an - gel - ic host pro - claim Christ is_____ born in Beth - le - hem.
Pleased as Man with man to dwell; Je - sus_____ our Em - man - u - el!

"Hark!" the her - ald an - gels sing, "Glo - ry_____ to the new - born King."

3. Mild He lays His glory by,
Born that man may no more die;
Born to raise the sons of earth,
Born to give them second birth.
Ris'n with healing in His wings,
Light and life to all He brings;
Hail, the Son of Righteousness!
Hail, the heav'n-born Prince of Peace!

Hark! the herald angels sing, etc.

50

THE HOLLY AND THE IVY

Another great find by the English folk song collector Cecil Sharp. It was collected in England in the early 1900s. Holly and ivy as part of religious festivals predates Christianity.

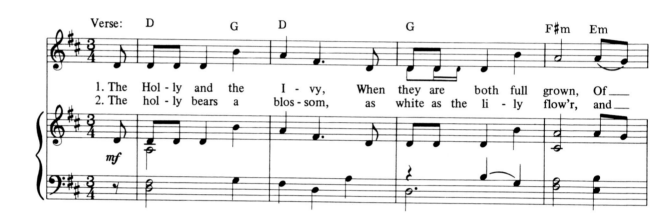

Verse:

1. The Hol - ly and the I - vy, When they are both full grown, Of___
2. The hol - ly bears a blos - som, as white as the li - ly flow'r, and___

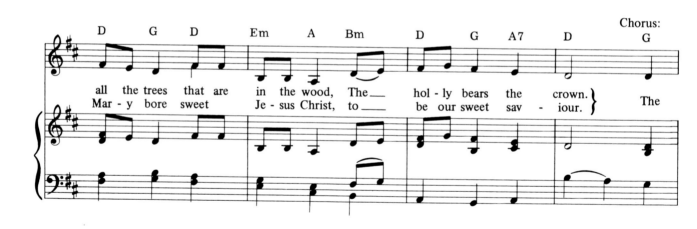

all the trees that are in the wood, The___ hol - ly bears the crown. }
Mar - y bore sweet Je - sus Christ, to___ be our sweet sav - iour. }

The

ris - ing of the sun,___ And the run - ning of the deer, The___

play - ing of the mer - ry or - gan, sweet sing - ing in the choir._____

3. The holly bears a berry
As red as any blood,
And Mary bore sweet Jesus Christ
To do poor sinners good.
(Chorus)

4. The holly bears a prickle
As sharp as any thorn,
And Mary bore sweet Jesus Christ
On Christmas Day in the morn.
(Chorus)

5. The holly bears a bark
As bitter as any gall,
And Mary bore sweet Jesus Christ
For to redeem us all.
(Chorus)

I HEARD THE BELLS ON CHRISTMAS DAY

WORDS BY HENRY WADSWORTH LONGFELLOW
ADAPTED BY JOHNNY MARKS   MUSIC BY JOHNNY MARKS

Johnny Marks wrote this popular Christmas song to his own adaptation of Henry W. Longfellow's words. Marks wrote several Christmas songs, the most famous of which is "Rudolph the Red-Nosed Reindeer," also in this collection. Bing Crosby introduced "I Heard the Bells" in 1956; some seventy other artists have also recorded it, including Placido Domingo and Frank Sinatra.

bel - fries of all Chris - ten - dom Had rung so long the un -
is not dead, nor doth He sleep, The wrong so long shall fall, The

bro - ken song Of peace on earth, good will to men.
right pre - vail, With

peace on earth, good will to men."

8va

rit.

I WONDER AS I WANDER

This exquisite folk carol was collected in the South in the 1930s by the singer and collector John Jacob Niles. His unusual countertenorlike voice in a collection recorded by RCA Victor before World War II was very influential in bringing old folk songs out of the hills to the attention of city folk.

1. I wonder as I wander out under the sky, How Jesus the Saviour did come for to die, For
2. When Mary bore Jesus, 'twas in a cow's stall, With wise men and shepherds and angels and all, And

poor or - n'ry peo - ple like you and like I, I
high from God's heav - en a star's light did fall, And the

won - der as I wan - der out un - der the sky.
prom - ise of a - ges it then did re - call.

3. If Jesus had wanted for any wee thing—
A star in the sky or a bird on the wing,
Or all of God's angels in heaven for to sing—
He surely could have it, for He was the King.

I'LL BE HOME FOR CHRISTMAS

WORDS BY KIM GANNON   MUSIC BY WALTER KENT

Another perennially favorite Christmas song, and deservedly so. There is something very touching about the idea that "I'll Be Home for Christmas, if only in my dreams."

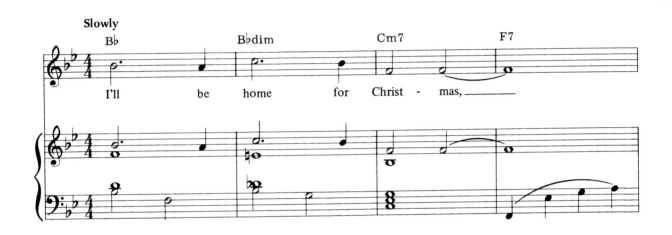

I'll be home for Christ - mas, _____

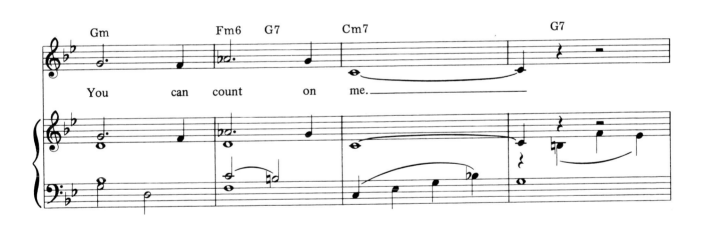

You can count on me. _____

Please have snow and mis - tle - toe And

on - ly in my dreams.

IN THE BLEAK MIDWINTER

Despite his Teutonic name, Gustav Theodore Holst, who wrote the music for this song, was an English composer of great originality, admired enormously perhaps more by musicians than by the general public. Christina Rossetti, who wrote the words, was also English, despite *her* name, and the sister of Dante Gabriel Rossetti, also a poet. She is regarded by some as the finest female poet in English literature.

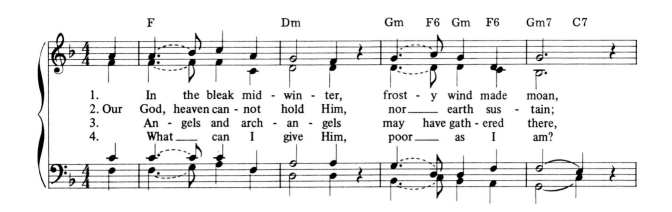

F   Dm   Gm   F6   Gm   F6   Gm7   C7

1.   In the bleak mid - win - ter,   frost - y wind made   moan,
2. Our God, heaven can - not hold Him,   nor____ earth sus - tain;
3.   An - gels and arch - an - gels   may have gath - ered   there,
4.   What____ can I give Him,   poor____ as I   am?

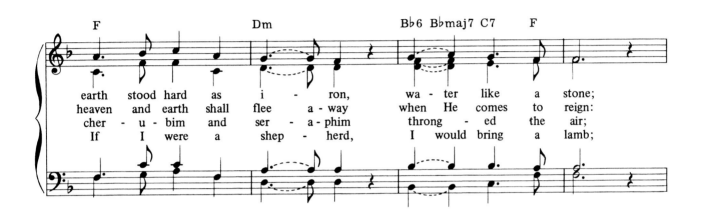

F   Dm   Bb6   Bbmaj7   C7   F

earth   stood hard   as   i - ron,   wa - ter like   a   stone;
heaven   and earth shall   flee   a - way   when He comes   to   reign:
cher - u - bim and   ser - a - phim   throng - ed   the   air;
If   I were   a   shep - herd,   I would bring   a   lamb;

Bb   F7   Bb   Dm   F   Am   Bb6   Bbmaj7   C   F

snow   had fall - en,   snow   on snow,   snow____ on   snow,
in   the bleak mid - win - ter   a   sta - ble - place suf - ficed,   the
but   His moth - er   on - ly   in her maid - en   bliss,
if   I were   a   wise____ man,   I would do my   part;   yet

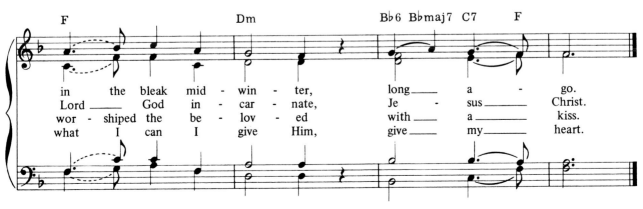

F   Dm   Bb6   Bbmaj7   C7   F

in   the bleak mid - win - ter,   long____ a -   go.
Lord____ God in - car - nate,   Je - sus____   Christ.
wor - shiped the be - lov - ed   with____ a____   kiss.
what   I can I give Him,   give____ my____   heart.

IT CAME UPON THE MIDNIGHT CLEAR

The composer did not write his melody for the words, but as a separate carol. The author of the words was a minister. The words and music appeared in the same year, 1850, but separately, and they were not put together until sometime later. Many sing it, "It came upon *a* midnight clear." The tune is also used often for the carol "While Shepherds Watched Their Flocks by Night."

1. It came up-on the mid - night clear, That glo - ri - ous song of
2. Oh, ye, be - neath life's crush - ing load, Whose forms are bend - ing

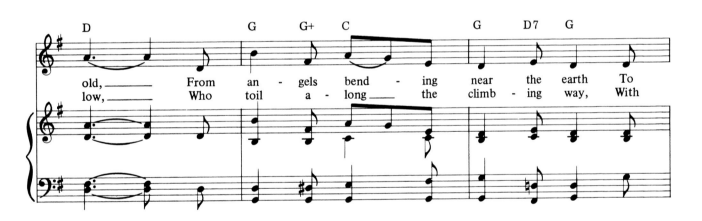

old, From an - gels bend - ing near the earth, To
low, Who toil a - long the climb - ing way, With

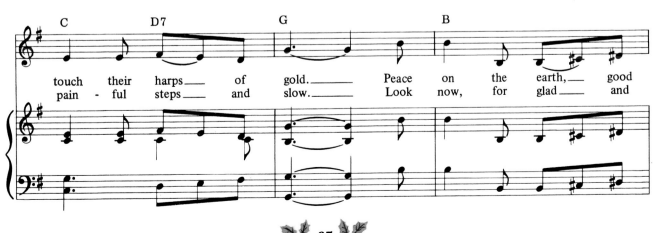

touch their harps of gold. Peace on the earth, good
pain - ful steps and slow. Look now, for glad and

will to men, From heav - en's all gra - cious King._____ The
gold - en hours Come swift - ly on _____ the wing, _____ Oh,

world in sol - emn still - ness lay, To hear the an - gels sing. _____
rest be - side ___ the wea - ry road, And hear the an - gels sing. _____

3. Still through the cloven skies they come
With peaceful wings unfurled,
And still their heavenly music floats
O'er all the weary world.
Above its sad and lowly plains,
They bend on hov'ring wing,
And ever o'er its Babel sounds,
The blessed angels sing.

4. For lo! the days are hastening on
By prophets seen of old,
When with the ever circling years
Shall come the time foretold:
When the new heav'n and earth shall own
The Prince of Peace, their King,
And the whole world send back its song
Which now the angels sing.

JINGLE BELLS

Of course, this is not a Christmas song, strictly speaking, but what would Christmas be without it? Written by John Pierpont (1785–1866), it is a song of winter that is always heard at Christmas.

Dash - ing thru the snow   in a   one - horse o - pen sleigh,

mf
(Melody)

fun it is to ride and sing a sleigh - ing song to - night!

Jin - gle Bells! Jin - gle Bells! Jin - gle all the way!

(Melody)

Oh! what fun it is to ride in a one - horse o - pen sleigh, Oh!

Jin - gle Bells! Jin - gle Bells! Jin - gle all the way!

Oh! what fun it is to ride in a one-horse o-pen sleigh! Hey!

JOY TO THE WORLD!

The tune is incorrectly credited to George F. Handel in some collections. The fact is that not only did he not write it, but no one knows who did. The words were published in 1719, in a work entitled *Psalms of David, Imitated in the Language of the New Testament.*

Joy to the world! The Lord is come. Let earth re-
Joy to the earth! The Sav - iour reigns. Let men their

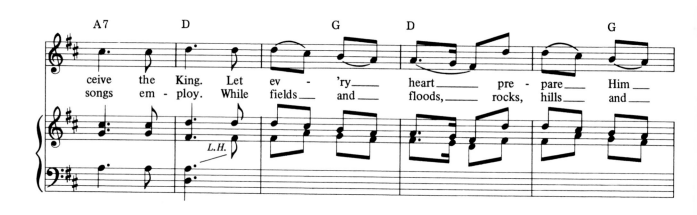

ceive the King. Let ev - 'ry___ heart___ pre - pare___ Him___
songs em - ploy. While fields___ and___ floods,___ rocks, hills___ and___

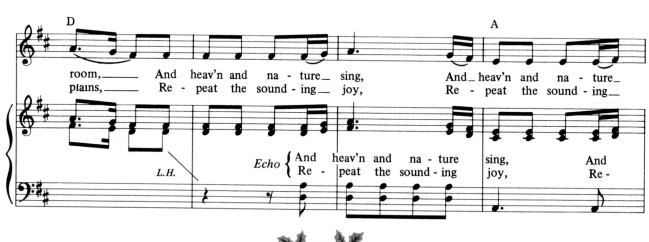

room,___ And heav'n and na - ture_ sing,   And_ heav'n and na - ture_
plains, ___ Re - peat the sound - ing_ joy,   Re - peat the sound - ing_

Echo { And heav'n and na - ture sing,   And
Re - peat the sound - ing joy,   Re -

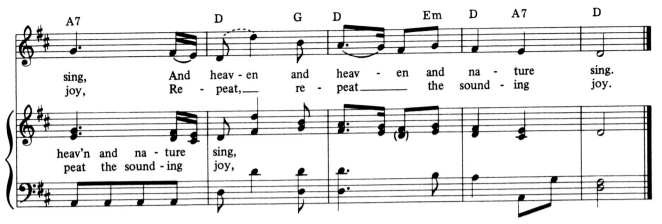

sing, And heav-en and heav-en and na-ture sing.
joy, Re - peat,___ re - peat___ the sound-ing joy.

heav'n and na-ture sing,
peat the sound-ing joy,

3. No more let sins and sorrows grow,
Nor thorns infest the ground.
He comes to make His blessings flow
Far as the curse is found; far as the curse is found,
Far as, far as the curse is found.

4. He rules the world with truth and grace
And makes the nations prove
The glories of His righteousness
And wonders of His love, and wonders of His love,
And wonders, and wonders of His love.

LITTLE BITTY BABY (GO, I WILL SEND THEE)

This is my adaptation of an American Negro folk carol. It was discovered in a church in the rural South, sung electrifyingly by an a-cappella male group with subtle, untutored, primitive, and very powerful harmonies and contrapuntal rhythms. I made the first commercial recording in the late forties or early fifties.

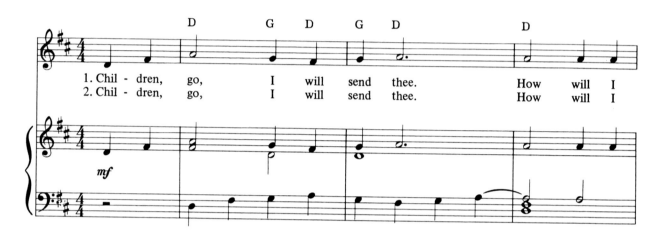

1. Chil - dren, go, I will send thee. How will I
2. Chil - dren, go, I will send thee. How will I

send thee? I'm a-gon - na send thee___ one by one.
send thee? I'm a-gon - na send thee___ two by two.

One's for the lit - tle bit - ty ba - by who's
Two's for Jo - seph and Mar - y

born,   born,   born in Beth - le - hem.

3.   Three's for the three old wise men; Two's for Joseph and Mary, etc.

4.   Four's for the four who stood at the door; Three's for the three old wise men, etc.

5.   Five's for the Hebrew children; Four's for the four . . . etc.

6.   Six for the six who had to get fixed; Five's for the Hebrew children, etc.

7.   Seven's for the seven who went to Heaven; Six for the six . . . etc.

LO, HOW A ROSE E'ER BLOOMING

According to the writer of the lyrics the rose is an imagined flowering, in the wintertime miraculously, of a branch from the roots of Jesse, based on the prophecy of Isaiah in the Old Testament, eight hundred years before Christ; the rose blooming every year symbolizes Jesus, of Jesse's lineage. The melody appeared in Cologne in 1600 and was later harmonized by Michael Praetorius; the words were printed (in German, of course) with the melody. Dr. Theodore Baker, who translated the words into English, was a very well known American musicologist. Note the unusual number of bars, seventeen, due to the irregular stresses of ancient melodies deriving from Gregorian chant or plainsong.

1. Lo, how a rose e'er bloom-ing from ten-der leaves hath sprung. From Jes-se's lin-eage com-ing, as men of old have sung. It came a flow'r-et bright, a-mid the cold of win-ter, when half spent was the night.

2. I-sai-ah 'twas fore-told it, the rose I have in mind. With Mar-y we be-hold it, as the Vir-gin Moth-er kind. To show God's love a-right, she bore to men a Sav-iour, when half spent was the night.

LULLY, LULLAY

(THE COVENTRY CAROL)

Robert Croo wrote the words over fifty years before the melody first appeared in the 1500s, for a Christmas pageant or "mystery" play. The melody comes from a time when bar lines didn't exist, and mixing of two-beat and three-beat cadences was common. Also, the melody is "modal," which means it is based on an older melodic scale different from our modern, simpler major or minor scales, just as in "Lo, How a Rose E'er Blooming," for example.

1. Lul - ly, lul - lay, Thou lit - tle ti - ny Child, Bye - bye, lul - ly, lul - lay. Lul - lay, Thou lit - tle ti - ny Child, Bye - bye, lul - ly, lul - lay.
2. O sis - ters too, how may we do, For to pre - serve this day, This poor young - ling, for whom we do sing, Bye - bye, lul - ly, lul - lay.

3. Herod, the king, in his raging,
Chargèd he hath, this day,
His men of might, in his own right,
All children young to slay.

4. Then woe is me, poor Child, for Thee,
And ever mourn and say
For Thy parting, nor say, nor sing
Bye-bye, lully, lullay.

O CHRISTMAS TREE (O TANNENBAUM)

The origin of this song, one of the best loved in Germany, is very obscure. The origin of the fir tree as a symbol of Christmas is also shadowy. Most of us, of course, will recognize the tune in the Civil War song "Maryland, My Maryland."

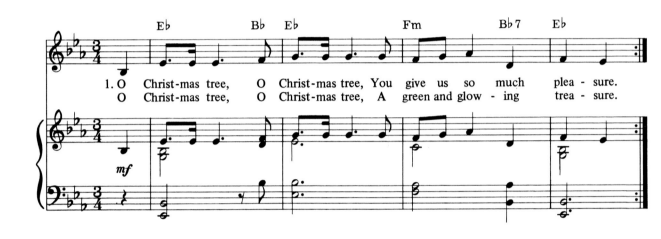

1. O Christ-mas tree, O Christ-mas tree, You give us so much plea - sure.
O Christ-mas tree, O Christ-mas tree, A green and glow - ing trea - sure.

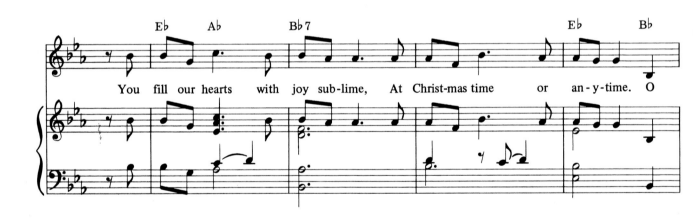

You fill our hearts with joy sub-lime, At Christ-mas time or an-y-time. O

Christ-mas tree, O Christ - mas tree, You give us so much plea - sure.

2.   O Christmas tree, O Christmas tree,
Forever green you're growing.
Not only summers are you green,
But in the winter's snowing.
O Christmas tree, from you I found
How Christmas lasts the whole year round.
O Christmas tree, O Christmas tree,
Forever green you're growing.

O COME, ALL YE FAITHFUL (ADESTE FIDELIS)

The Latin words could well have been written by John F. Wade, an Englishman exiled in France, in the 1740s. The music is ascribed to a John Reading, an organist of the sixteenth century. The English words are by various hands. It has always fascinated me that the Latin words have persisted so stubbornly and are sung very often.

1. O come, all ye faith - ful, joy - ful and tri -
2. Sing choirs of an - gels, sing in ex - ul -
Ad - es - te fi - del - is, lae - ti, tri - um -

um - phant, O come ye, O come ye to
ta - tion, Sing. all ye cit - i - zens of
phan - tes, Ve - ni - te, ve - ni - te in

Beth - le - hem; Come and be -
heav'n a bove; Glo - ry to
Beth - le - hem. Na - tum vi -

3. Yea, Lord, we greet Thee, born this happy morning;
   Jesus, to Thee be glory giv'n;
   Word of the Father, now in flesh appearing;
   O come, etc.

84

O COME, O COME, EMMANUEL

The melody is, in my view, not only one of the most beautiful of all Christmas songs but of all melodies. It is some eight hundred years old, a type known as plainsong from the days before the invention of bar lines. Emmanuel, or Immanuel, as it is sometimes spelled, means "God with us," according to the prophet Isaiah, who prophesied the virgin birth and the son of God, so that Emmanuel is another name for Jesus.

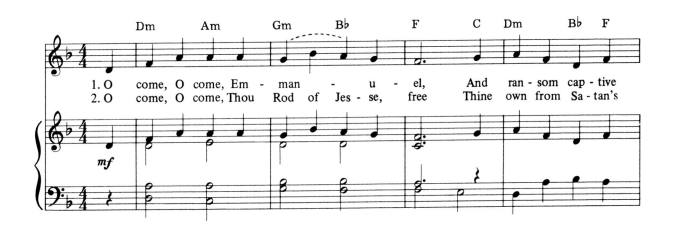

1. O come, O come, Em - man - u - el, And ran - som cap - tive
2. O come, O come, Thou Rod of Jes - se, free Thine own from Sa - tan's

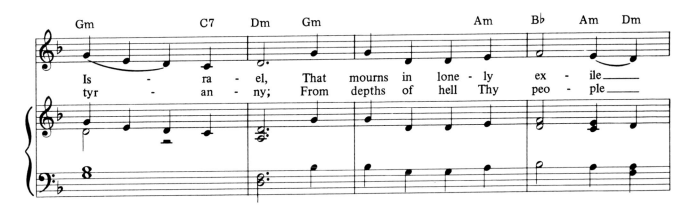

Is - ra - el, That mourns in lone - ly ex - ile
tyr - an - ny; From depths of hell Thy peo - ple

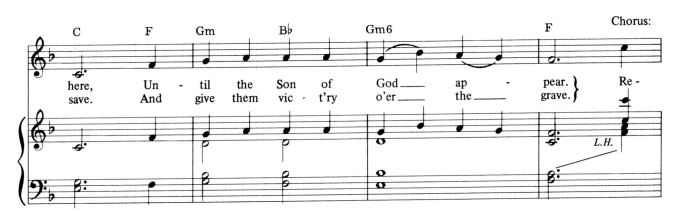

here, Un - til the Son of God ap - pear. } Re -
save. And give them vic - t'ry o'er the grave. }

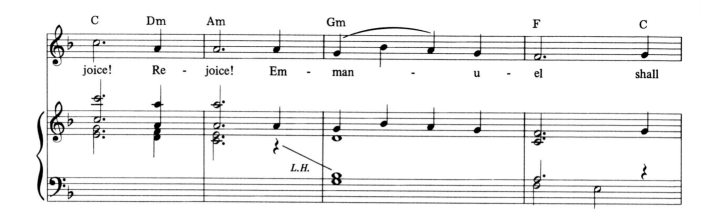

joice! Re - joice! Em - man - u - el shall

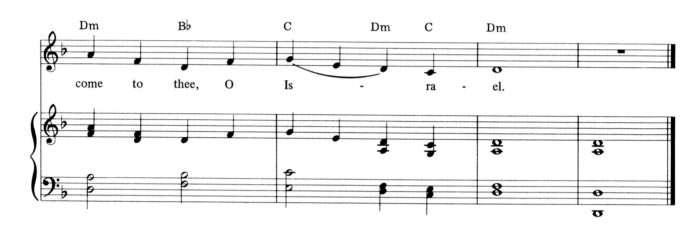

come to thee, O Is - ra - el.

3. O come, Thou Dayspring, come and cheer
Our spirits by Thine advent here;
Disperse the gloomy clouds of night,
And death's dark shadows put to flight.
(Chorus)

4. O come, Thou Key of David, come,
And open wide our heav'nly home;
Make safe the way that leads on high,
And close the path to misery.
(Chorus)

5. O come, O come, Thou Lord of might,
Who once, from Sinai's flaming height,
Didst give the trembling tribes Thy law,
In cloud, and majesty, and awe.
(Chorus)

O HOLY NIGHT (CANTIQUE DE NOËL)

Despite the fact that many people of "elevated" musical tastes—whatever that means—along with even some members of the Catholic hierarchy at times, have regarded this song as "corny" or even irreligious, it remains immensely popular with millions of people. Adolphe Adam, the composer, is also known today for his enduring ballet, *Giselle*. The English translator was a minister, Rev. J. S. Dwight.

O Ho - ly Night, _____ the stars are bright - ly shin - ing; _____ it is the night of our dear Sav - iour's birth. _____ Long lay the world, _____ in sin and er - ror pin - ing, _____ and He ap -

O LITTLE TOWN OF BETHLEHEM

Phillips Brooks was one of the most influential clergymen of his time, especially in Boston. He became bishop (Episcopal) of Massachusetts. While at Holy Trinity Church in Philadelphia, he wrote the words. It is said he had been inspired three years earlier by a Christmas trip on horseback from Jerusalem to Bethlehem. In any case, the words were set to music by his organist, Lewis H. Redner, and the song was introduced at Christmas in a Sunday school class.

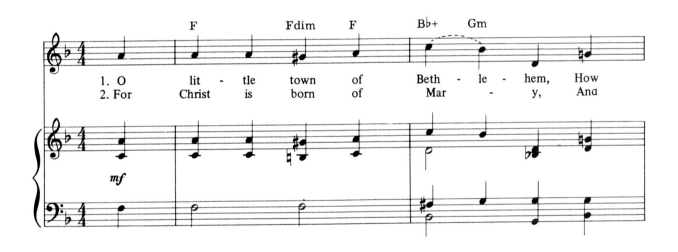

1. O lit - tle town of Beth - le - hem, How
2. For Christ is born of Mar - y, And

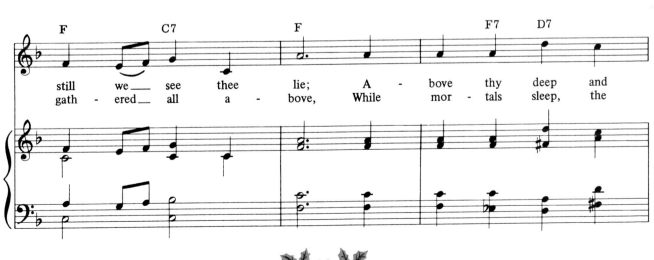

still we — see thee lie; A - bove thy deep and
gath - ered — all a - bove, While mor - tals sleep, the

3. How silently, how silently,
The wond'rous gift is given;
So God imparts to human hearts
The blessing of His heaven;
No ear may hear His coming,
But in this world of sin,
Where meek souls will receive Him still,
The dear Christ enters in.

4. O holy child of Bethlehem,
Descend to us, we pray,
Cast out our sins, and enter in,
Be born in us today;
We hear the Christmas angels
The great glad tidings tell;
Oh come to us, abide with us,
Our Lord Emmanuel.

PATAPAN

This charming carol first saw the light in 1842 in France—at least the earliest surviving printed copy dates from that time. I have supplied my own translation, having had a longtime love affair with French and my native tongue, English.

Wil - lie drum a rum - tum - tum, Then_Rob - in's fife will

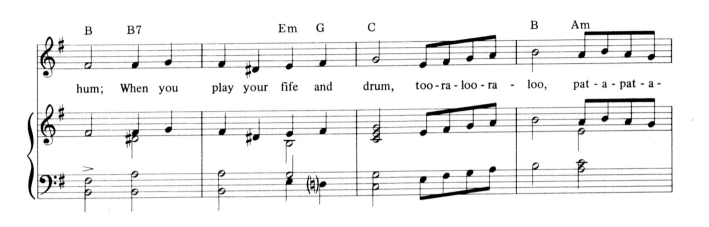

hum; When you play your fife and drum, too - ra - loo - ra - loo, pat - a - pat - a -

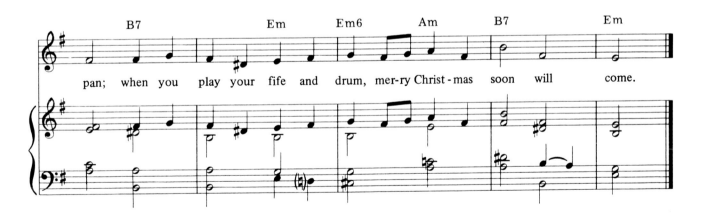

pan; when you play your fife and drum, mer - ry Christ - mas soon will come.

2. From olden times, glad happenings
To praise the King of kings
When you play, etc.

3. God and man become as one
More than your fife and drum
When you play, etc.

RUDOLPH THE RED-NOSED REINDEER

WORDS AND MUSIC BY JOHNNY MARKS

Who would have thought that Santa's traditional reindeer in "The Night Before Christmas" would acquire such an amazingly popular addition? In 1949, Gene Autry was persuaded to record this song after many record companies had emphatically turned it down. And what did Johnny Marks, who wrote it, name his publishing company, which was created by the huge success of "Rudolph"? St. Nicholas Music, Inc., what else?

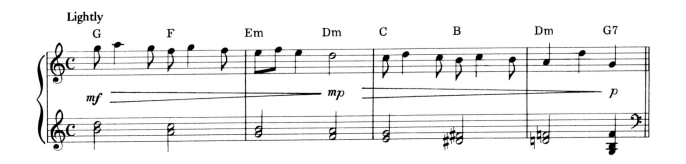

Lightly

Verse: *(ad lib)*

You know Dash-er and Danc-er and Pranc-er and Vix-en, Com-et and Cu-pid and

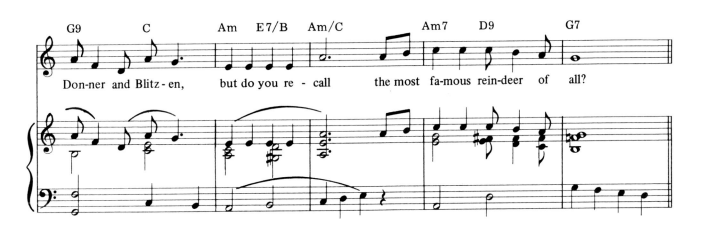

Don-ner and Blitz-en, but do you re-call the most fa-mous rein-deer of all?

Refrain: *(a tempo)*

Ru-dolph, the red-nosed rein-deer had a ver-y shin-y nose,

99

and if you ev - er saw it, you would e - ven say it glows.

All of the oth - er rein - deer used to laugh and call him names,

they nev - er let poor Ru - dolph join in an - y rein - deer games.

Then one fog - gy Christ - mas Eve, San - ta came to say,

THE SEVEN JOYS OF MARY

There are a number of versions of this folk song, varying both in lyrics and in melody. This is one of the better ones, I think, collected in the southern United States in the 1930s.

Verse:

1. The ver - y first bless - ing that Mar - y had, It was the bless - ing of
2. The ver - y next bless - ing that Mar - y had, It was the bless - ing of

one, To think that lit - tle Je - sus Was God's on - ly Son,
two, To think that lit - tle Je - sus Could read the Bi - ble through, Could

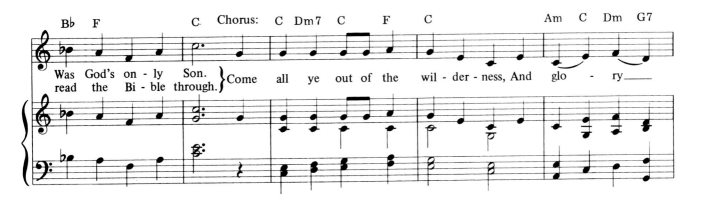

Was God's on - ly Son.
read the Bi - ble through. } Come all ye out of the wil - der - ness, And glo - ry ___

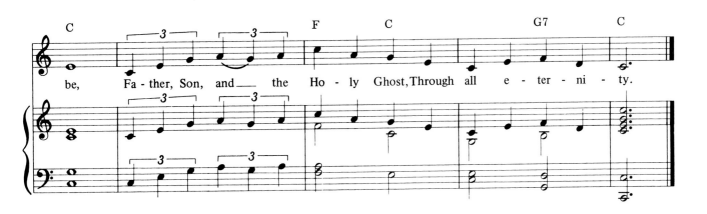

be, Fa - ther, Son, and ___ the Ho - ly Ghost, Through all e - ter - ni - ty.

3. The very next blessing that Mary had,
It was the blessing of three:
To think her little Jesus
Could make the blind to see,
Could make the blind to see.
(Chorus)

5. The very next blessing that Mary had,
It was the blessing of five:
To think her little Jesus
Could make the dead to rise,
Could make the dead to rise.
(Chorus)

4. The very next blessing that Mary had,
It was the blessing of four:
To think her little Jesus
Could make the rich to poor,
Could make the rich to poor.
(Chorus)

6. The very next blessing that Mary had,
It was the blessing of six:
To think her little Jesus
Could make the well to sick,
Could make the well to sick.

7. The very last blessing that Mary had,
It was the blessing of seven:
To think that her son Jesus
Had gone away to heaven,
Had gone away to heaven.
(Chorus)

SILENT NIGHT

If there is one carol that could be called the most beloved of all, it undoubtedly must be "Silent Night," written for the Christmas holiday in 1818, in Oberndorf, Austria. The words are by Joseph Mohr, the assistant minister of the church, and the music by Franz Gruber, an occasional organist.

1. Si - lent night, ho - ly night! All is calm, all is bright,
2. Si - lent night, ho - ly night! Shep - herds quake at the sight!

Round yon Vir - gin Moth - er and Child, Ho - ly In - fant so ten - der and mild
Glo - ries stream from heav - en a - far, Heav'n - ly hosts sing al - le - lu - ia;

Sleep in heav - en - ly peace, Sleep in heav - en - ly peace.
Christ the Sav - iour is born! Christ the Sav - iour is born!

3.
Silent night, holy night!
Child of Heav'n, oh how bright;
Thou didst smile when Thou wast born!
Blessed be that happy morn,
Full of heavenly joy,
Full of heavenly joy!

THE TWELVE DAYS OF CHRISTMAS

As I wrote in a previous book about this wonderful song: A great "cumulative" song, that is, one in which the verses accumulate as they are sung. It has become so well known in the past forty years that we see it on napkins, Christmas cards, and almost anywhere else—which doesn't spoil it at all. The first recording in this country was made by the author in 1945. Recently, there was some talk that the song was written as a "catechism in code for persecuted Catholics in sixteenth-century England," but scholars are dubious.

1. On the first day of Christ-mas my true love gave to me a

par - tridge__ in a pear tree.__ On the sec - ond day of Christ - mas my

true love gave to me two tur - tle doves and a par - tridge__ in a pear

tree.__ On the third day of Christ - mas my true love gave to me

three French__ hens, two tur - tle doves, and a par - tridge__ in a pear

me five gold___ rings, four___ col - ly birds, three French hens, two___ tur - tle doves, and a par - tridge___ in a pear tree._____ On the sixth day of Christ-mas my true love gave to me six geese a - lay-ing, five gold___ rings, four___ col - ly birds,

Verses 6-12

three French hens, two_ tur-tle doves, and a par-tridge_ in a pear tree.___

7. Seven swans a-swimming . . .

8. Eight maids a-milking . . .

9. Nine pipers playing . . .

10. Ten ladies dancing . . .

11. Eleven lords a-leaping . . .

12. Twelve fiddlers fiddling . . .

WASSAIL SONG (HERE WE COME A-WASSAILING)

The noun "wassail" means a festive drink; the verb means, interestingly enough, both to make or have a festive drink of wassail, say at Christmas, and merely to go singing from door to door at Christmas. Singers would often be given a drink for their efforts. The custom still goes on; I have gone a-wassailing on cold, clear, beautiful nights, and even in the snow. This wassail song (there are others) may have come from the North of England in the seventeenth century.

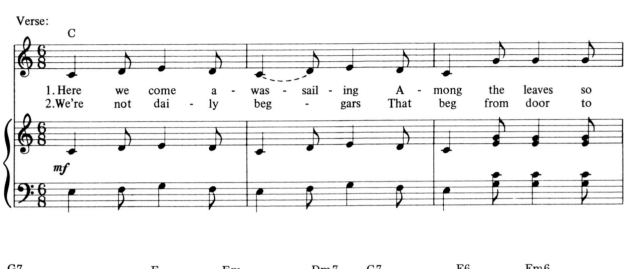

1. Here we come a - was - sail - ing A - mong the leaves so
2. We're not dai - ly beg - gars That beg from door to

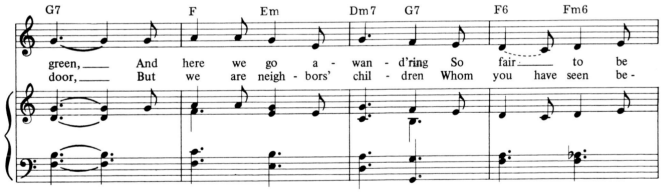

green,___ And here we go a - wan - d'ring So fair___ to be
door,___ But we are neigh - bors' chil - dren Whom you have seen be -

seen. } Love and joy come to you, and to you, your was - sail,
fore. }

too, and God bless you and send____ you a hap - py New

Year, and God send you a hap - py New Year. ____

3. Call up the butler of this house;
Put on his golden ring;
Let him bring us a glass of beer,
And better we shall sing.
(Chorus)

4. We have got a little purse
Of stretching leather skin;
We want a little money
To line it well within.
(Chorus)

5. Bring us out a table,
And spread it with a cloth;
Bring us out a moldy cheese,
And some of your Christmas loaf.
(Chorus)

6. God bless the master of this house;
Likewise the mistress too,
And all the little children
That round the table go.
(Chorus)

7. Good master and good mistress,
While you sit by the fire,
Pray think of us poor children
A-wand'ring in the mire.
(Chorus)

WE THREE KINGS

Many have noted that the style of the melody seems to place it as a medieval tune, but it was written in the 1850s by an interesting minister who wrote music and poetry and even designed stained glass, as well as heading various churches. He was John H. Hopkins.

We three kings of O - ri - ent are; Bear - ing gifts we trav - el a - far; Field and foun - tain,

MELCHIOR: Born a king on Bethlehem's plain,
Gold I bring to crown Him again;
King forever, ceasing never,
Over us all to reign.
(Chorus)

CASPAR: Frankincense to offer have I;
Incense owns a Deity nigh;
Pray'r and praising, all men raising,
Worship Him—God most high.
(Chorus)

BALTHAZAR: Myrrh is mine, its bitter perfume
Breathes a life of gathering gloom,
Sorrowing, sighing, bleeding, dying,
Seal'd in the stone-cold tomb.
(Chorus)

ALL: Glorious now behold Him arise,
King and God and sacrifice;
"Alleluia, alleluia,"
Earth to the heav'ns replies.
(Chorus)

WE WISH YOU A MERRY CHRISTMAS

An English street carol that became popular here with the great wave of city interest in folk songs in the late 1930s. As is the case, alas, with many, many folk songs, no one knows its origin; it just "appeared," fortunately for all of us.

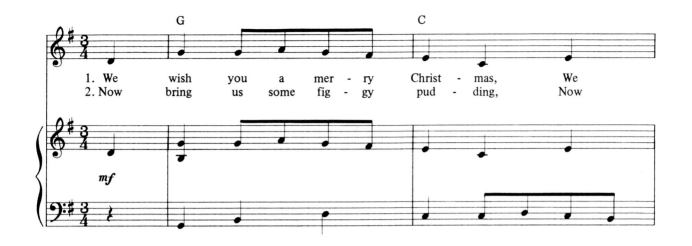

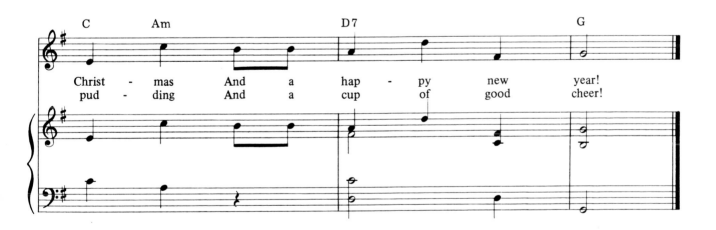

3. We won't go until we get some,
We won't go until we get some,
We won't go until we get some,
So bring it out here.

4. (Repeat first verse.)

119

WHAT CHILD IS THIS?

The tune is, of course, "Greensleeves," mentioned in Shakespeare's *The Merry Wives of Windsor;* it is one of the very greatest melodies in Western music. The writer of the words was both a writer of hymns and an insurance company executive, from Bristol, England. The words appeared during Queen Victoria's long reign.

1. What child is this,___ who laid to rest___ On Mar - y's lap___ is
2. Why lies He in___ such mean es - state,___ Where ox and ass___ are

sleep - ing? Whom an - gels greet___ with an - thems sweet,___ While
feed - ing? Good Chris - tians fear,___ for sin - ners here___ The

shep - herds watch___ are keep - ing. } This, this___ is Christ the King,___ Whom
si - lent Word___ is plead - ing. }

Chorus:

shep - herds guard ___ and an - gels sing. This, this ___ is Christ the King, ___ The babe, ___ the son ___ of Mar - y.

3. So bring Him incense, gold, and myrrh;
Come, peasant, king to own Him.
The King of kings salvation brings;
Let loving hearts enthrone Him.
(Chorus)

INDEX OF FIRST LINES